Bermuda Rock Lessons

by

Ezra Ararat

Ezra Ararat
Paget
Bermuda
Printed in Canada

Fax: 441-232-1496

ISBN: 1-896441-27-0

Dedication

To my sons Ezra 1 and Ezra 2.

For listening and for their inspiration, many thanks to Mr. Wendell Gibbons, Mr. Glenn Shorto and all the wonderful children who spend their summers at The Coral Beach Club.

Acknowledgments

The author would like to thank The Writers' Machine and its team of creative experts: Dale Butler, Marcus Tucker, Kathleen Gamble and Bobie Christmas.

Table of Contents

Billy the Super Ant

his is a story about how Billy the ant got his nickname, Super Ant.

As you know, ants move around in armies. Years ago, Grandfather ants traditionally took their grandsons and daughters to watch the march of the soldier ants. Two days before Billy was going to join the army, his grandfather walked him down to the parade grounds to watch the march.

Billy sat beside his grandfather and asked question after question, never waiting for answers, just chattering on and on, excited to be part of the great tradition.

Suddenly, a large object appeared near Billy and his grandfather. The other ants shouted, "It's a stick! It's a stick!"

Billy and his grandfather raced to safety. Out of breath, Billy asked, "What in the world is that, Grandpa?"

"There's something I need to tell you about the outside world," his grandfather answered. "There are giants out there. The bigger ones, parents, don't attack us, unless we interfere with them, but the smaller ones, called children, have fun crushing us."

Billy's little body shook in fear, but the little ant's grandfather reassured him. "Don't be afraid; be prepared," his grandfather offered. "We have to live with human beings. Just two weeks ago, I was taking my afternoon walk, when I saw Mrs. Bee collecting nectar. She warned me that the giant children were hunting for ants. I thanked her and told her to be careful as well. She laughed and told me they would never bother her or her hives again, because Mr. Bee had taught one of them a lesson.

"She told me, 'I was home alone protecting my babies a week ago, when Johnny the kid came along and swatted me off my hive. Tommy the ant saw what happened and pulled me into the high grass, out of sight.' She wiped a tear from her eye, when she talked. 'Through the grass, Tommy and I watched as Johnny destroyed my nest and killed my babies.'

"Tommy tended Mrs. Bee's wounds and dried her tears, she told me, and later, when Mr. Bee returned, he found her crying, sitting on the bare branch where their hive once had been.

"Her husband was upset when he saw that their nest was destroyed and their babies gone, Mrs. Bee said. When she told her husband what happened, he grew angry. He sharpened his stinger and flew to Johnny's house and waited. When Johnny walked out, he was eating an ice cream cone. Mr. Bee flew down Johnny's shirt and stung him all over his belly. Mrs. Bee told me Johnny cried for two days."

Billy grabbed his own stomach and rubbed it. "Boy, I'll bet that hurt."

"Pain was just part of it. Guess what happened next."

Billy's eyes grew wide. "What?"

"Well, I'll tell you." Billy's grandfather told Billy that Mrs.

Bee overheard Johnny's parents talking, and they said he was allergic to bee stings. "Yes, he can't ever go near a bee again." The older ant laughed. "He learned a lesson he'll never forget."

Billy nodded, thinking about the story his grandfather had told him.

Billy's grandfather yawned. "It's time for my nap," he said and wandered down the ant hole.

Billy rubbed his chin and continued to consider all that he had learned. He thought about the stick that had frightened him. He wondered if the giant children who crushed ants with their sticks could also be taught a lesson they would never forget. He got up to have a talk with Mr. Bee.

On his way, Billy passed soldier ants who were back on the job. They had carried the injured ants away, and they were again defending their kingdom and protecting the army ants who brought food.

Once away from his kingdom, Billy stood all alone in an unfamiliar world. His gaze roamed around, and the sights amazed him. He saw a giant dog running across a lawn, and he grew frightened, but he remembered that his grandfather had told him not to be afraid, but be prepared. Billy prepared himself to bite anything that got in his way.

Thunderous laughter surprised Billy. He looked across the freshly cut grass and

saw three giant children with sticks, crushing ants. Billy's little heart raced, but he was not afraid.

Determined to teach those giants a lesson they would never forget, Billy marched on, his chest out and his head held high. He passed thousands of ants trying to escape the giant children. They shouted to Billy, "Run! You've got to get out of here!" Billy shook his head, pursed his little lips and kept marching.

Up ahead, Sue the cat extended her claws and stretched, scraping at the ground. She narrowly missed Billy, but Billy was not afraid. He saw other ants being tossed around like dust, and he called out at the top of his voice, "Stop! You're crushing my people."

The cat continued to scratch the earth.

Some ants fled for their lives; others lost theirs.

Billy took a deep breath, jumped as high as he could, and landed on the cat's paw. He opened his jaws and sank his little teeth into the paw.

The cat let out a loud, pained meow. Billy jumped to safety, and the cat ran off.

All the ants that had fled came back and thanked Billy.

Some followed him as he continued his march across the lawn toward the giant children.

When Billy reached the youngsters, he hollered, "Stop that!"

They ignored him and kept drilling their sticks into the ground on either side of him.

He took a deep breath, leaped into the air and landed on one of the giant's shoes. Billy quickly crawled up the boy's leg and bit him. The giant screamed, dropped his stick, and ran towards home. Billy bounded off, took another deep breath and vaulted onto the other giant child, who had stopped drilling with his stick and was watching with astonishment as his friend ran off screaming.

Billy crawled all the way to the boy's bellybutton and bit as hard as he had ever bitten before. The second child sprang about four feet into the air and turned toward home, shrieking at the top of his lungs.

Billy quickly leaped off and made his way to the last boy, who stood speechless. Before Billy could reach him, the child dropped his stick and fled. Billy grabbed the boy's trailing shoelace and hung on. Away they went, ant and boy, all the way home.

When the child reached his house, he sat down to rest, huffing and puffing.

While the boy tried to catch his breath, Billy crawled around until he found a soft, fat place where he also rested awhile.

When the giant caught his breath, he let out a great sigh. Billy took that moment to sink his teeth into the boy's fat flesh. The boy bellowed so loud he almost lost his voice.

Billy hung on with his teeth, while the child ran around and around in circles, screaming.

Exhausted, Billy dropped to the ground. He relaxed for a time before making his way back home, a silly smile on his face. The last bite was the best, he kept thinking.

Billy reached home just in time for supper. No one had missed him. He took one bite of his food, and his head dropped into his plate.

His mother stood with her hands on her hips. "You've done nothing to prepare yourself for the world, and now you're too tired to stay awake. Go to bed."

The little ant stood and started to walk to his room, but his grandfather stepped up. "Wait." The grandfather turned to his daughter. "He's a good ant, really."

Billy's mother shook her head. "He's got only one day left before he joins the army, and what has he done? Wasted the whole day."

Billy's father interrupted. "All the ants are talking about a super ant that defeated a giant cat and three giant kids."

The grandfather smiled. "If that's true, it's the greatest thing that ever happened. Does anyone know where the super ant came from?"

"No," said Billy's father, "but a scout was following his trail, and is supposed to report back, soon."

A knock came from the front of their house, and Billy's mother answered it. A scout stood in the doorway. "I have some odd news, folks." He shook his head slowly. "The super ant isn't from the outer world; he lives right here in our kingdom." He looked around and pointed to Billy. "In fact, that's him, right in your own house. That's him, the super ant!"

Billy's father walked over to the little ant that stood with his head dropping to his chest. "Billy, are you the super ant that defeated a giant cat and not one, but three giant kids?"

"Yes, Father, it is true. Billy rubbed his weary eyes.

"I've told you never to leave this kingdom, Billy's mother declared. "You could have been killed."

Billy looked up at his mother, a tear in his little eye. But Grandpa told me not to be afraid; to be prepared."

"It's my fault." The grandfather moved forward. "I told Billy the story of how Mr. Bee taught Johnny a lesson, and he must have decided to do something no ant has ever done before."

Billy's mother hugged the little ant. "Billy, you're a super son."

The scout nodded." Yes, and a super ant."

"Super ant!" everyone cried out. Billy had the nickname for life.

The End

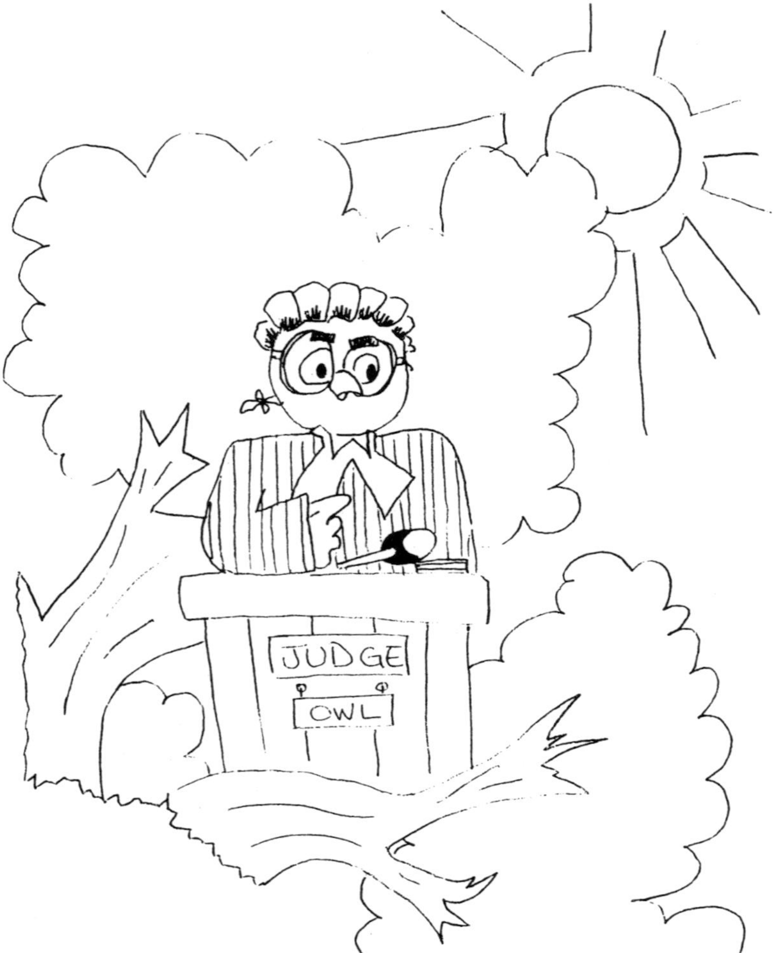
JUDGE
OWL

The Calabash Tree

A calabash tree once grew in a yard in Flatts near the drawbridge. When someone committed a crime, the judge sentenced the guilty party under the calabash tree, where all could see. Mr. Owl, the judge at that time, along with his assistant, Mrs. Longtail, sentenced the last animal under that old tree in 1943.

The police had charged Mr. Redbird, Mr. Bluebird, and Mrs. Sparrow with eating Mrs. Earthworm's babies while they were playing in Mr. Burchall's garden. Each suspect gave a statement.

Mr. Redbird spoke first. "I was busy gathering bark from a dead cedar tree near Mr. Burchall's garden, and I didn't notice anything was wrong until I heard Mrs. Earthworm crying for her babies."

Mrs. Sparrow said she was near Mr. Burchall's garden eating Mexican peppers. "I didn't hear or see a thing," she testified.

When Mr. Bluebird took the stand, he said, "I was singing a melody on a cedar branch that grew next to Mr. Burchall's house, and I didn't hear or see anything, either."

Mr. Owl and Mrs. Longtail listened carefully to what each of the suspects had to say. They spoke in hushed tones until they chose the guilty party.

Mr. Owl explained, "We both agreed it couldn't have been

Mr. Redbird, because his mouth was full of bark for his nest. It couldn't have been Mrs. Sparrow, either, because she was still eating Mexican peppers. Mr. Bluebird is the guilty one, because a bird always sings after eating a meal."

The judge pointed. "Mr. Bluebird, this court finds you guilty of eating Mrs. Earthworm's children. We will all meet under the calabash tree tomorrow at sunrise, at which time I will announce your sentence."

The next day, the sun climbed from behind Castle Harbour Hotel, sending dancing rays of orange light on the currents that swept under Flatts Bridge. Spectators from every parish in Bermuda packed the courtyard.

Mr. Owl and Mrs. Longtail stood under the calabash tree awaiting the arrival of Mr. Bluebird. He arrived bound in chains. Mr. Cat stood on one side of him, and Mr. Rooster positioned himself on the other side. The crowd parted as Mr. Cat and Mr. Rooster led Mr. Bluebird to the calabash tree. The trio stopped in front of Mrs. Longtail.

She glared at the guilty bird. "Mr. Bluebird, do you have anything to say?"

Mr. Bluebird dropped his beak and shook his head from side to side.

Members of the crowd waved their fists in the air. Spectators shouted, "Hang him!" "String 'im up!"

Mr. Owl raised his hand and demanded silence. "Mrs. Longtail and I have agreed there will be no more hangings from the calabash tree. Instead, we have sentenced Mr. Bluebird to a life of awaking at dawn and singing from the branch of a cedar tree until the sun rises over Castle Harbour.

Rumbles ran through the gathering, but soon everyone nodded in agreement, including Mrs. Earthworm.

If you are ever awakened by a song so blue it makes you want to cry, look out your window. You will see a bluebird sitting on the branch of a cedar tree. Try not to shed a tear, but if you do cry, cry for Mrs. Earthworm's babies that Mr. Bluebird grabbed up as they played in Mr. Burchall's garden.

The End

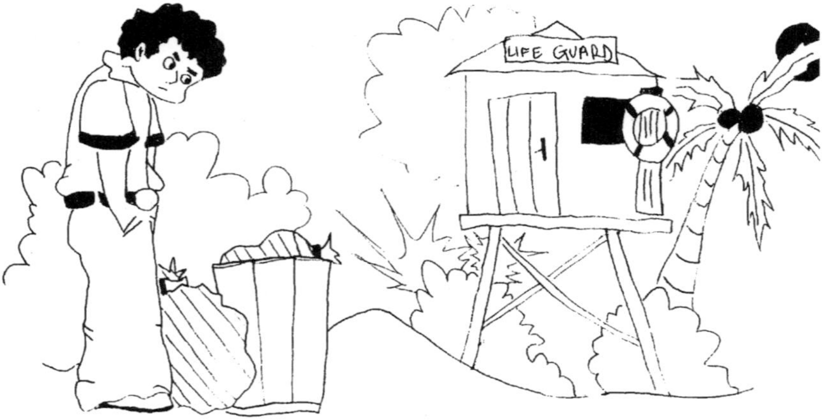
LIFE GUARD

The Little Trash Boy

ay was small, for a thirteen-year-old, and had a hard time finding a summer job. Everywhere he applied, someone would look at him and say, "You look too small to handle this job." The only job he could find was picking up trash at his favorite beach, where all his friends played throughout the summer.

The first week he went to work, he combed the beach for trash, but no matter where he walked, people teased him. The boys called him "Little Trash Boy," and the girls held their noses when he walked by.

Early one morning, while Ray picked up trash, the senior lifeguard walked up. "Little Trash Boy, could you assist me today? Andrew can't make it; he has the chicken pox."

Ray looked up at the towering lifeguard. "Are you sure you want me, Mr. Gray?" the little boy asked.

"Yes," said the lifeguard.

"Oh, boy!" Ray shouted. He hurried to clean the beach early. When his friends arrived, Ray wanted to be sitting in Andrew's lofty chair.

As people wandered out onto the beach, Ray sat high in Andrew's chair, wearing sunglasses. Beside him sat a six-pack of Pepsi. Several boys gathered around the chair. One of them roared,

"Look at the tiny trash boy; he finished cleaning the beach, and now he's looking for more trash in the ocean." The boy shook Ray's chair, and Ray had to hold on tight to keep from falling.

Mr. Gray saw the children and hurried over, hollering for the boy to stop. All the boys ran off, laughing.

Mr. Gray looked at Ray. "Is everything all right?"

"Yes," the boy said from on top of his tall platform. "Thank you." Ray looked away, to keep from showing his embarrassment.

"Ray, I know it's hard being a trash boy; I was one myself." The lifeguard patted Ray on the foot. "Look on the bright side. You're getting paid, and you're helping God keep the earth clean. With God on your side, you're on the right track."

Ray smiled. He felt confidence for the first time in his life.

As the hours passed, the wind blew harder. The waves rolled over, making a thunderous roar, when they broke.

Mr. Gray came up to Ray's lifeguard chair and pointed at the water. "It's getting dangerous out there. I'm going to the lifeguard shack to get the red flag. We need to put it up and get the children out of the water. You watch things while I'm gone."

"Yes, sir," Ray said.

After Mr. Gray left, Ray heard loud cries and screams from the shoreline. Ray squinted out over the ocean and saw a little child being carried out to sea. Without hesitation, Ray jumped down from his chair, ran to the water and dived in. Ray swam through wave after wave, determined to save the child, but even as Ray swam, the undertow carried the child out farther.

Ray swam, stroke after stroke, pulling his body through the thundering, crashing water, until he reached the child and pulled him back to shore safely.

Everyone clapped with joy.

Mr. Gray was so delighted he gave Ray a summer job as a lifeguard for as many summers as Ray wanted.

From that day forward, no one called Ray the little trash boy. Everyone called him "Brave Ray."

The End

Porky's Night Out

One warm July night, the stars shone brightly. Porky had looked forward to that night ever since his birthday, two months earlier. Early that morning, he had packed the new knapsack that had been a birthday gift from his mother. He had enough food to last at least three days.

Careful not to wake his parents, who were sleeping in the next room, Porky climbed out of his window, his knapsack flung over his right shoulder. In his left hand, he carried Marcus, the teddy bear that had been his friend since Porky was a baby. Together they had planned to run away from home.

Porky ran quickly from his yard and looked back only once to see if anyone had heard him leaving. The house was still in darkness. He breathed a sigh and walked towards the bright lights of the city. He was only a block from his house, when he heard a bang. He almost jumped out of his skin. He jerked around to find that a garbage can had fallen on the pavement. Porky started to run down the street, but a voice called out, "Hey, you!"

Porky stopped and looked around, but saw no one.

The voice called again. "Hey, you."

Porky bent over. The voice seemed to come from the garbage can, but the boy knew garbage cans couldn't talk, and that one didn't seem big enough to hold a person. Porky walked over to the garbage can, anyway.

A head popped out of the can, and Porky froze.

"Don't be afraid of me," the head said. "You should be afraid of him."

"Who?" Porky shook all over.

"Your parents never told you?" the head asked.

"No, my parents only tell me to clean my room, eat my vegetables, and do my homework. I'm tired of listening to my parents, and I've run away."

"So your parents didn't tell you, and now you've run away. Hoo, hoo, well, don't feel left out; my parents never told me, either. I had to run away to find out."

Porky's voice quivered. "Find out what?"

"It was a night just like tonight, when I ran away. That's when I found out."

The boy rubbed his ears. A head in a garbage can was talking to him. Curiosity overcame his fear.

"Go on."

The head continued, "Yes, the night I ran away, a voice called out to me from a garbage can, just like I called you. Just like you, I walked over to look inside, and I was scared stiff, too, just like you."

Porky's eyebrows rose. "And what did you see inside the garbage can?"

"I found the biggest hand I'd ever seen. It popped out and pulled me in, and it began to eat me. It didn't stop until it ate almost every last bit of me."

"You expect me to believe that?" Porky laughed. "If you were eaten up, you wouldn't be able to talk to me."

"You're right." The head nodded. "But as you see, the hand didn't eat all of me. He left enough so that every night, I could eat little boys like you, who run away from home."

Porky leaped back. He turned and ran for his life. His little feet didn't touch the ground until he reached his house and climbed back inside his window. As he lay in his safe bed that night, he decided his parents were okay after all, and he promised himself he would never again run away from home.

The End

Snake Lessons

Dogger the snake lived by a lake with his sister Jane and his Aunt Kate. Dogger was a prankster who thought it fun to fool others.

One spring morning, Dogger crawled through some mangrove trees that surrounded the lake. He saw his Uncle Thon, who had the strength of twenty snakes, hanging from a branch. Dogger thought about how much respect and admiration he would get from his friends, if he could trick Uncle Thon. While Dogger watched, his uncle's stomach gave a loud, rumbling growl. "Hmmm," Dogger said. "That gives me an idea."

Dogger called to his uncle, "I'm on my way to feast on the fattest white rats you've ever seen. I know how much you love white rats. Would you like to join me?"

"This isn't one of your pranks, is it?" Uncle Thon glared down at his nephew.

"Honest to King Cobra, I'm telling the truth." If Dogger had fingers, he would have crossed them.

Uncle Thon swayed back and forth in the breeze. "Oh, okay, I'll join you." He slid down the tree.

Dogger crawled from one mangrove branch to another, while Uncle Thon followed. In a little while, Dogger stopped. "It's not that I don't trust you, Uncle Thon, but I think the sight of so many rats may be too tempting for you. You'll want to eat them all, and if you did, you'd make yourself sick." Dogger acted as though he were thinking for a moment. "Why don't you stay here, while I go and bring you back a dozen?"

Uncle Thon tore a leaf from one of the branches and covered his mouth.

"I should have thought of that," Dogger squealed. "We snakes use our tongues to sense chemical particles in the ground and air. With your tongue covered, you won't be able to sense the rats as much, so you won't be as tempted to overeat. Follow me." He led his uncle up close to a beehive. "Stand here," Dogger said. He shook the branch, slithered away, and jumped into the lake.

The bees flew out of the hive in a huff, and when they saw Uncle Thon, they attacked and stung him all over.

Uncle Thon writhed in pain, crying out, "Have mercy! Have mercy!"

The bees ignored him and continued to attack.

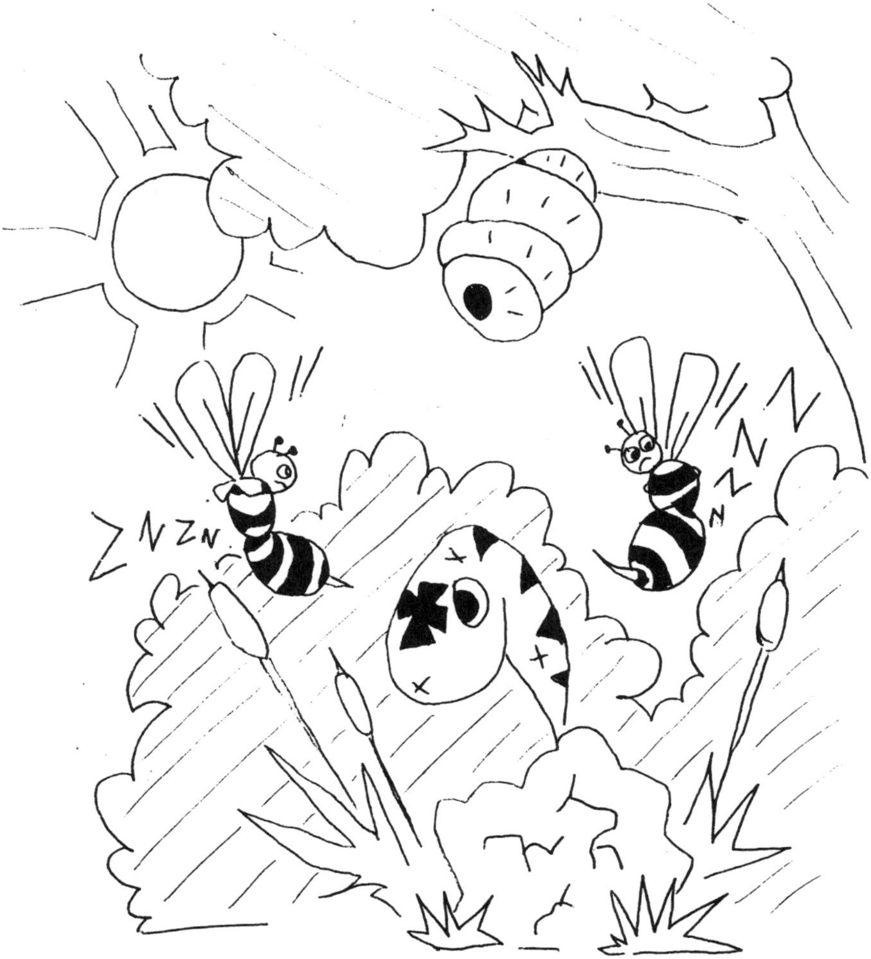
ZNZN
NZNZ

Word spread that Dogger had pulled a painful prank on his strong Uncle Thon, and Dogger's friends treated him like royalty. His sister Jane and Aunt Kate were not at all pleased with Dogger's trick, though. They visited Uncle Thon and found him in the lake, soaking his stings.

Jane apologized for her brother. "I don't know why he does such mean things, Uncle Thon. Surely he understood it would hurt."

Aunt Kate splashed water on the hurting snake to cool off the stings that burned like fire.

On the way home, Jane and Aunt Kate found Dogger being carried around by friends. Dogger called out, "Do you want a ride?"

Jane hissed, and the two continued on their way, not even gazing at Dogger.

Aunt Kate spoke out of the side of her mouth. "It's about time someone taught that Dogger a lesson," she said.

Jane nodded. "I was thinking the same thing."

Aunt Kate stopped in her tracks. "But how do you trick a trickster?"

When Jane whispered her plan to her aunt, Kate let out an uncontrollable laugh.

"Sh-h-h, Dogger might hear us," Jane warned.

Dogger saw the two women whispering and moved closer, slowly and quietly, so he could hear what they were saying.

"Luckily, Thon has the strength of twenty snakes, or he would not have lived through all those bee stings," Kate said. "I'm going to pick some special leaves tomorrow morning, so Thon can put them on his stings to ease the pain. Would you like to join me, Jane?"

"Yes, I'd loved to help. Are those the magical leaves Uncle Thon uses to get his super strength?"

Before Kate could answer, Dogger ran up. "May I come?"

Jane did not answer.

Aunt Kate scowled. "Haven't you done enough damage for one day?"

The pair slithered off without Dogger.

That night was a restless one for Dogger. His mind spilled over with mischief. He thought that once he found the magical leaves, he would eat them all, and no one would be able to tell him what to do, anymore. He awoke early the next morning and waited for Kate and Jane to leave; he followed them for a distance.

They crawled to a part of the lake where Dogger had never been. The pair stopped by a big mangrove tree, and Kate pointed to a huge tree with large leaves covered with red spots. She and Jane gathered a few leaves and turned to leave. When they looked back, they saw Dogger hungrily munching on the leaves.

Dogger ate as many leaves as his stomach could hold. Bloated, he lay on a branch and waited for the magical leaves to work and make him as strong as or stronger than his Uncle Thon. Time passed, but he did not feel stronger. Instead, he felt something bite him on his stomach. More bites followed. The pain became so unbearable he cried out for help.

Aunt Kate and Jane snickered.

"The 'magical leaves' are working," Jane said.

Kate smiled. "Dogger won't be stronger, but he'll learn a lesson."

In pain, Dogger rolled over and coughed, and hundreds of red ants spilled out of his mouth. He coughed again, and more red ants came out. "Oh, no! Those weren't magical red spots," Dogger moaned. "They were stinging ants."

On their way back home, Aunt Kate and Jane told everyone about Dogger and the red ants. Everybody laughed.

From that day on, Dogger never again played a trick on anyone. He had learned a valuable lesson: Never trick anyone, especially those you love and trust and those who love and trust you.

The End

The World Rulers

Four great kings once ruled the four corners of the world. Each king thought he was greater than the other three, and each wanted to steal the other's crown and land.

One day, a wise old owl devised a solution to settle the kings' differences. She offered to set tasks for each king, and whichever proved himself superior win the other kingdoms.

All the kings eagerly agreed, including the ant king from the East, the spider king from the West, the bee king from the South, and the fly king from the North.

Each king believed his unique gift was the most important gift to have. The ant king could lift seven times his own weight; the spider king could spin an inescapable web, the bee king had a mighty sword, and the fly king took pride in being the greatest pest.

Mrs. Owl welcomed the kings to the competition and gave each a separate task.

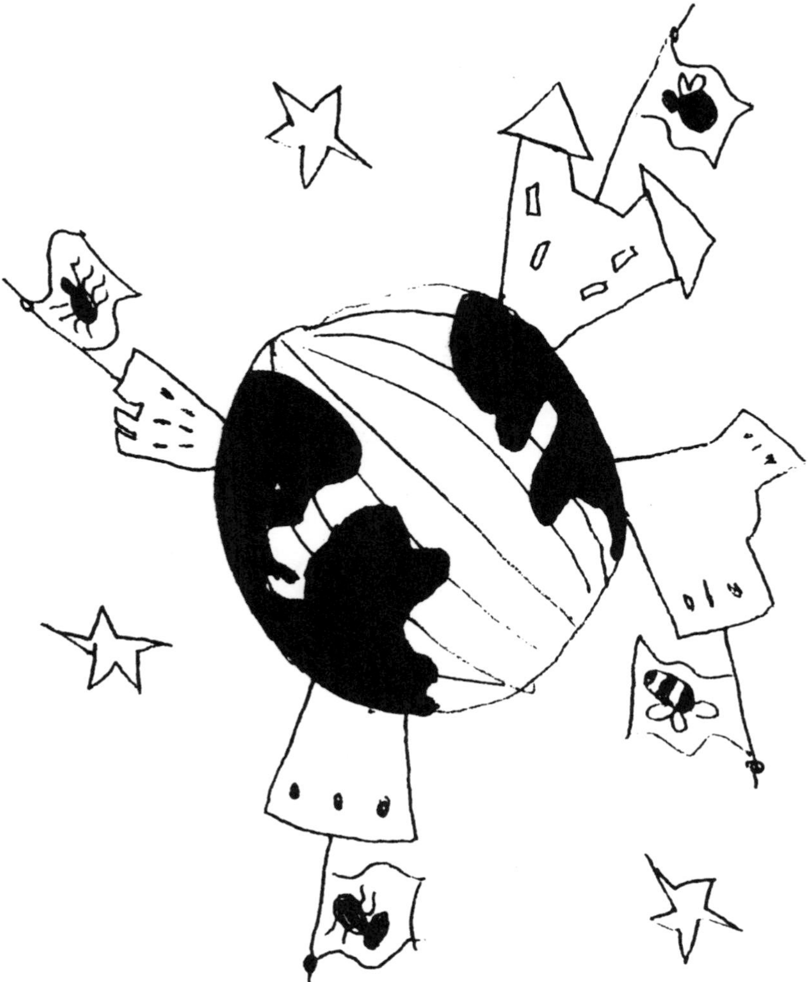

She challenged the ant king to fly like a bee and swing a mighty sword. She told the bee king to lift seven times his weight. To the spider king, she set the task of becoming the greatest pest, whilst the fly king had to spin an inescapable web.

Each king set off to complete his assigned chore.

The ant king tried to fly like a bee, but he kept falling on his face. He even threw himself off a huge rock, but he merely succeeded in getting a lump on his head. He certainly could not figure out how to fly and swing a sword at the same time.

The bee king stepped up to some barbells and lifted his entire weight.

"Not good enough," said the owl. "You have to lift much more."

The bee king added to his load and lifted two times his own weight.

"You must lift seven times your weight," the owl said.

Try as he might, the bee king could lift not one bit more than twice his own weight.

The spider king tried to become a pest by shooting webs in every direction, but the webs did not bother anyone.

Instead, the spider king became entangled in his own webs and had to fight to get free.

The fly king grunted, groaned, hummed, and shook, but he could not make spider silk, and therefore had no way to make a web. He grew so frustrated that he became even more of a pest than ever.

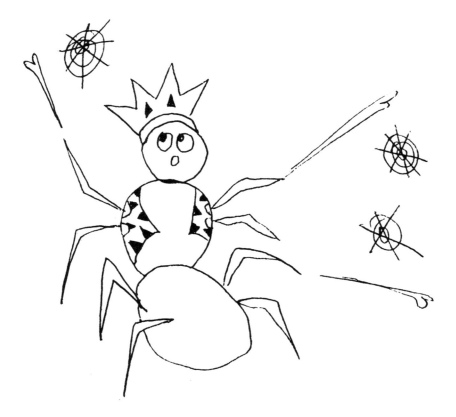

Frustrated and discouraged, the fly buzzed over to the spider. "You claim to be so wise. Why can't we do such simple tasks?"

The spider answered in a tired voice, "It seems that what is simple for one can be impossible for another."

The kings looked enviously at each other, jealous they could not perform each other's tasks.

The bee king wept, for even with his mighty sword, he could not lift seven times his weight. The ant king crawled over and soothed the bee king. "Don't cry. Maybe if I help you and you help me, we can rule half the world."

The fly flew up. "Hey," he said. "If the spider and I work with you, the four of us can rule the whole world."

Mrs. Owl smiled. "You see now that teamwork can change the world. You have proved you can't change who you are, but you can change what you do."

Ever since that time, the ant, the spider, the bee, and the fly have ruled the insect kingdom the world over.

The End

Spider Bridge

Ants once were very lazy. They never did anything except play in the grass and sleep under the sun. A special ant named Milky, though, learned the rewards of hard work, and he changed everything in the ant world.

A river ran through the ant kingdom and brought them the water they needed. Over a section of the river, a sinister structure called Spider Bridge stretched from one bank to another. The bridge had existed for more than a hundred years, and thousands upon thousands of spider webs clung to its surfaces. Ants never tried to cross the bridge, because they all had heard stories of ants who tried to cross and never returned.

Milky grew up near Spider Bridge, and never stepped foot on its ancient timbers, but his friend Spike caught Milky staring at the structure one day. Spike walked up close and said in a low tone, "I just heard that anybody who crosses that bridge will find the wisest spider in the world."

"We already know spiders are the wisest of creatures, so what's so special about the one on the bridge?" Milky asked.

Spike stared into his friend's eyes. "Think about it. They're already wise, and this one is even wiser. Think of

SPIDER Bridge

all she must know! I heard that if she sees somebody brave enough to cross the bridge, she'll teach him how to attain wisdom."

"What a gift that would be!" Milky touched his chin. "I'm already braver and smarter than most of the other ants. I'm going to cross that bridge and learn even more."

Milky stepped toward Spider Bridge, looked back and saw Spike still standing in the same place. Milky called, "Come and look."

Spike stepped forward, but he saw all the spider webs and stiffened.

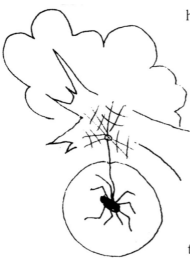

"Wish me luck," Milky said as he put one foot on the old wood of the bridge.

"Good luck." Spike waved from a few feet back.

Milky had not walked far, when several little spiders dropped from their webs. One of them shouted, "Where do you think you're going?"

"I'm going to reach the other side." Milky pointed to the far end of the bridge.

The spider sneered. "You can try, but you won't succeed." All the spiders shot webs at Milky, but their webs did not stop the brave little ant. He gnawed his way through.

Spike trailed behind his friend, unnoticed.

With determination, Milky continued until he was halfway across the bridge. The spiders finally ceased their attacks, and Milky ventured forward more easily. Soon his way grew more difficult as the old webs covering the bridge got stronger and stickier. He still managed to cut his way through to the last web. He came face to face with the evil Golden Silk Spider. The large spider said in a deep voice, "You have come far, little ant, but you will go no farther." He fired a strong web of silk and pinned Milky to the bridge. The spider laughed. "Stay there while I come and give you a little bite."

Spike could watch no longer. He leaped out and ripped at the bonds holding his friend. The Golden Silk Spider turned, the golden patches on his back glistening in the sun.

He roared in anger and shot a web at Spike. The poor ant became hopelessly entangled. The Golden Silk Spider cackled at the helpless ant.

Quietly, Milky freed himself from the webbing and crept up behind the spider. Before the Golden Silk Spider could react, Milky bit one of the spider's legs. The spider screamed, toppled back and fell through a crack in the bridge. The rushing water swept him away.

Milky freed Spike, and they crossed the bridge together. When the pair reached the end, a rush of wind gently blew the webs all about them. They brushed the webs out of their eyes and saw a shiny black widow spider sitting on a single strand of glistening silk.

She spoke in a gentle voice. "Welcome, brave friends. You have earned my advice. The way to wisdom is through teamwork, hard work, the setting of goals and the striving to achieve them. You have proven this by crossing the bridge. Now you know how to achieve any goal."

Milky said, "You mean everybody already has . . . "

His friend finished, ". . . the wisdom inside them?"

The dark spider nodded her wise head. "Right."

Milky motioned to Spike. "Let's go home and tell all the other ants what we learned."

They did, and now you no longer see ants playing in the grass or sleeping beneath the sun. Ants always work together as a team, and they stay busy, because they have learned the wise way to attain any goal.

The End

The Rubber Tree Oath

Kiskadees, those plump little birds, were not brought to Bermuda for their colour or their beauty. They were brought here to eat lizards. Lizards, which also are attractive, were not brought to Bermuda for their beauty, but to eat insects. Some people wonder why the kiskadees stopped eating lizards. The reason lies behind a story about a lizard named Nicky.

Nicky lived with her parents and two brothers in a rubber tree near Francis Patton School. Life on the rubber tree was pleasant. The fathers often sat on the high branches and displayed their orange throat flashes while they watched little children playing in the school yard. The mother lizards went about her chores, without having to worry about their babies. With the arrival of the kiskadees, though, everything changed.

Kurt led the flock of kiskadees. All lizards feared all kiskadees, but the leader—some called him Killer Kurt— was the most feared of all. He could catch a lizard in midair as it jumped off branches, trying to escape.

Because of Kurt, Nicky's parents no longer allowed their children to climb to the top of the rubber tree, where Kurt could see them and catch them easily. The children obeyed their parents for a long time, but after a while, life became boring for the little lizards. They longed to climb high in the tree and watch the children play in the school yard.

One windy day, a branch of the rubber tree cracked and almost fell off the tree. The sticky gum from the broken branch slowly oozed out and flowed all the way to the ground.

Nicky and her brothers were playing at the bottom of the tree, when they heard a shout that Killer Kurt was coming. Like a jet, Kurt flew around the rubber tree. All the lizards on the tree changed from deep brown to bright green, to blend in with the colour of the leaves. Kurt could not see any lizards, so he flew to the top of the tree, landed on the cracked branch, and looked left and right.

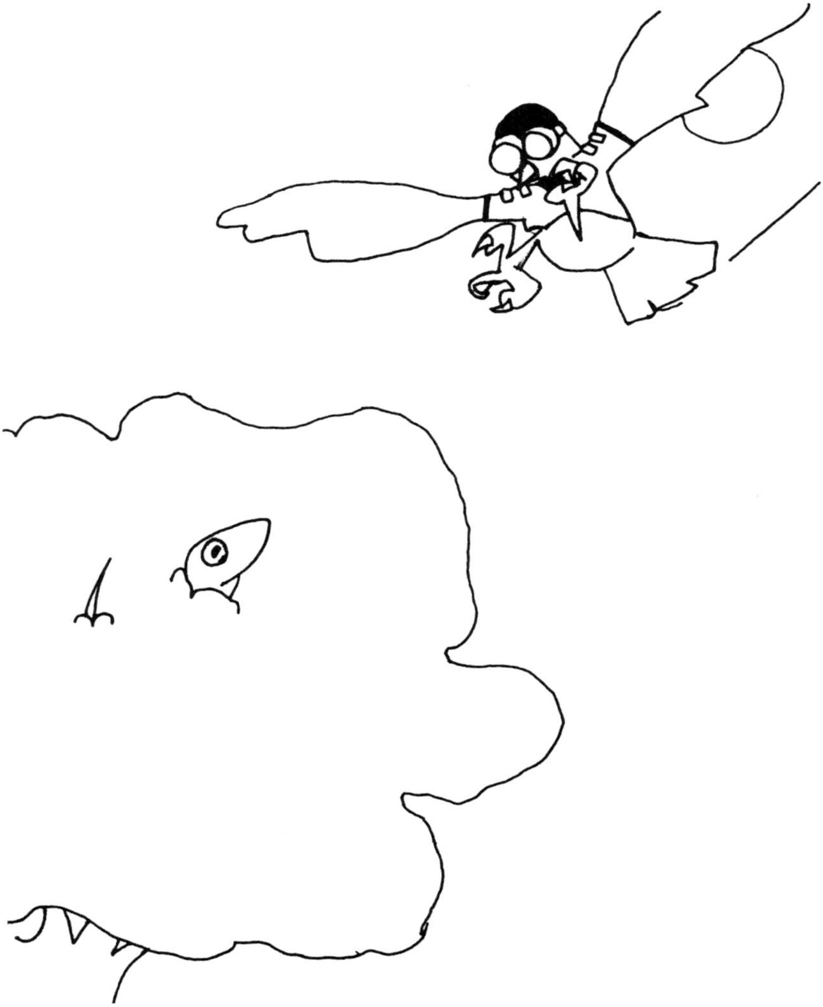

Nicky peeped at Kurt from under the leaf where she was hiding. She had never seen such a bright yellow bird. Her gaze met Kurt's, and the bird lurched forward, ready to dart down and gobble up Nicky. When Kurt tried to fly, however, he couldn't move. The gum from the rubber tree had hardened and glued the bird's feet to the branch. He struggled and pulled, but could not free himself. He called out, "Help!"

Other kiskadees came to assist Kurt, but not one of them could free the trapped leader.

One by one, the kiskadees left, and by the time dusk fell, Kurt was all alone. Hungry and thirsty, he hung his head, too exhausted to hold it up.

Nicky and her brothers were tucked away under the branches for the night, but Nicky could not sleep. She kept thinking about the helpless bird stuck in the rubber of the tree. She crawled up the rubber tree to see the stranded bird.

She finally reached the broken branch where Kurt wept softly.

"Hello," Nicky said.

Kurt raised his head a little. "Who are you?"

"I'm Nicky," the lizard replied.

"Have you come to watch me die?" Kurt blinked back a tear. "Are you happy I'm stuck?"

"No." Nicky shook her green head. "I really feel sorry for you."

Kurt stared at Nicky. "I thought all lizards were bad. You're different from other lizards."

"That's funny. First, not all lizards are bad. Most of us are quite nice. Second, I always thought all kiskadees were bad, but I find you quite nice."

The bird chuckled softly. "I guess we both made

incorrect assumptions. Kiskadees aren't all bad, either."

"I'm going to get you loose," Nicky said.

"What can a little lizard do? All my bird friends tried to help and failed."

Nicky flicked out her tongue. "They just didn't know what to do," she said. Nicky crept closer and licked at the rubber gum. Hour after hour, she licked, while Kurt watched and talked. Kurt told her about kiskadees and about other tropical birds. Nicky learned a great deal about her feathered friends.

When the sun peeped over Francis Patton School, a tired Nicky took one last, long lick, and Kurt flapped his wings and flew into the sky.

"I'm free! You are truly a saint," Kurt called down from the sky. "I'm making an oath that a kiskadee will never again hunt a lizard."

From that day on, the lizard population grew, and the kiskadees learned to eat Mexican peppers, instead of green and brown lizards.

The kiskadee remains one of the most colourful birds in Bermuda.

The End

Miracle

Sally, a colourful parrot fish, lived in the crystal blue waters of Coral Beach and fed on the scattered reefs. Sally wished she could join the children as they played on the beach. Sometimes she built sand castles on the sea floor, but the currents washed them away, every time.

When the weather was cool, she watched a boy and girl riding along the beach on a handsome black horse, and she quaked in fear when a wave spooked the horse and, threw off its two young riders. The boy stood, brushed the sand from his knees and ran over to the little girl, who did not move. The boy ran away, screaming for help, and soon people came and carried the little girl away. The boy sadly led the horse home, and Sally wondered if the little girl would be all right.

To her delight, when the weather turned warm, Sally saw the boy and girl on the beach again. This time, the boy wheeled his sister in a wheelchair, and although surrounded by children who played around her, the girl looked sad. Sally wondered why the girl did not join the children, so she decided to find out.

She slapped the surface of the water several times with her tail, and soon succeeded in getting the little girl's attention. The child smiled when she saw the parrot fish in the water. Sally continued to swim around and flap her tail, to the little girl's delight. At the end of the day, the girl's brother finished playing with his friends. "It's time to go home, " he said and he grabbed the handles on the back of the girl's wheelchair. The girl spoke with great excitement while Sally watched the pair leave the beach.

The next weekend, the girl brought bread crumbs to feed her new friend.

Sally flapped her tail for the little girl all day, but the girl sat in the chair. Sally wondered why the girl would not run and jump with the other children or sit on the sand and build castles. She listened carefully to the children's conversations, and gradually learned that the boy was named Johnny, and that her newfound friend was named Melissa.

Melissa looked grateful to have such as unique friend as Sally the parrot fish, which made Sally very happy. Their friendship continued for months. Sally grew pleasantly plump on all the snacks Melissa brought to feed the fish. Still, Sally longed to go up onto the beach and play with Melissa. She wanted to show Melissa how to build sand castles, how to play with friends. While Melissa threw bread crumbs to Sally one weekend, Sally simply stared at Melissa and pondered what she could do to make Melissa want to play with her. She stopped eating and stopped flapping her tail. She simply thought and thought, eyeing the little girl and wondering what to do next.

Melissa called from the beach, "What's wrong, little fish? Why aren't you swimming around? Why won't you eat?"

Sally opened and closed her mouth, and thought and thought some more. Finally the answer came to her. She took a deep breath and swam towards the shoreline until half her body was out of the water.

Melissa leaned forward. "You can't come out!" she shouted. "It's bad for you up here."

Sally shook her head and would not listen. She struggled out of the water and flapped until she moved farther and farther up on the beach.

"No! Go back!" Melissa cried.

Sally finally reached the wheelchair and threw herself at Melissa's feet. So delighted at the touch of her friend's toes, she flapped back and forth on the little girl's feet, having a wonderful time.

The water in her gills soon drained out, though, and Sally could not breathe. She stopped flopping and lay gasping at Melissa's feet.

Melissa screamed, "Johnny! Help!"

Johnny had run down the beach with his friends, though, and could not hear his sister's call.

"I can't walk," Melissa cried. "The doctors said I'll never walk again. You've got to go back in the water, where it's safe. I can't help you." She called for her brother again.

At last Johnny heard his sister's cries for help. He turned around, but he had far to go, to reach her. He grabbed his mouth and his eyes grew wide when he saw his sister push herself out of the wheelchair, stand, pick up Sally, and carry her to the sea.

She released the fish in the water, sobbing, "Please don't die, little fish."

Sally weakly flapped her tail back and forth. Gradually, her tail moved faster and grew stronger. Soon the little fish swam circles around Melissa, waving her fins happily.

When Melissa waded back to the beach, Johnny and his friends crowded around her, cheering and clapping. Johnny hugged his sister. "You can walk again. It's a miracle."

From the water, Sally smiled and flapped her tail at her good friend.

The End

The Wishing Well

The people who lived in Black Watch Pass needed water, so they built a well. From then on, they always had water to drink, even if it didn't rain for weeks on end.

Eight-year-old Tommy did not care about rain or even water. He knew the well was dug in the ground just for him. He called it his wishing well.

Tommy lived with his mother and five sisters in a house near Black Watch Pass. The family was poor. Many nights, all seven of them drank a glass of water for dinner and went to bed hungry.

Although other children rode the bus to school, Tommy and his sisters had to walk all the way to West Pembroke Primary. On cold days, the wind from the north shore almost blew the children away. On hot summer days, they longed for the cool winds of winter.

Every day, Tommy stopped by the well on his way to and from school, to make a wish. On Mondays, he always had a penny, which he had saved from Sunday School. He stood with his back to the well, holding his penny in his right hand, his eyes squeezed shut. "I wish my family wasn't poor," he said every time. "I wish Mother didn't have to work so hard." To complete his wish, Tommy threw the penny over his left shoulder, and would not turn around until he heard the coin splash into the water below.

Despite Tommy's efforts, his wishes never came true. That is, not until a very special Christmas Eve.

On that special Christmas Eve, Tommy walked to the well by himself. Tears rolled down his cheeks. He walked up and said, "I'll give it one more try."

Tommy turned his back, at the exact moment a big butterfly with bright blue wings landed on the well behind him, but Tommy did not see it.

Instead, he squeezed his eyes shut and lifted his right arm. Before he tossed his penny over his left shoulder, he stopped. "I'm changing my wish," he said. He paused and thought for a second. "Please, wishing well, please make my family happy this Christmas," he pleaded. "Please make my family happy this Christmas." He repeated his wish over and over, hoping someone would hear him.

Someone did. The butterfly heard him and followed Tommy home. She knew that once she winked her eye and made Tommy's wish come true, her life would end.

That night, while everyone in Tommy's house slept, the butterfly pressed against the windowpane and winked her eye. Poof! A Christmas tree, filled with strings of popcorn and cranberries, appeared in the living room. Presents overflowed from under the tree. A stuffed turkey filled the oven. Apples, oranges, potatoes, cakes, and breads filled the kitchen, enough to feed Tommy's family for a week.

The next morning, Tommy and his sisters squealed with delight when they saw the Christmas tree and all the presents. His mother smelled a turkey and ran into the kitchen. When she opened the oven, she cried with joy to see all the good food, piping hot and ready to feed her family.

Tommy looked up at his mother with a big smile on his face. "This is the happiest day of my life," he told her.

As he tore open his gifts, no one, not even Tommy, noticed the butterfly still pressed up against the window pane, with both eyes closed.

The End

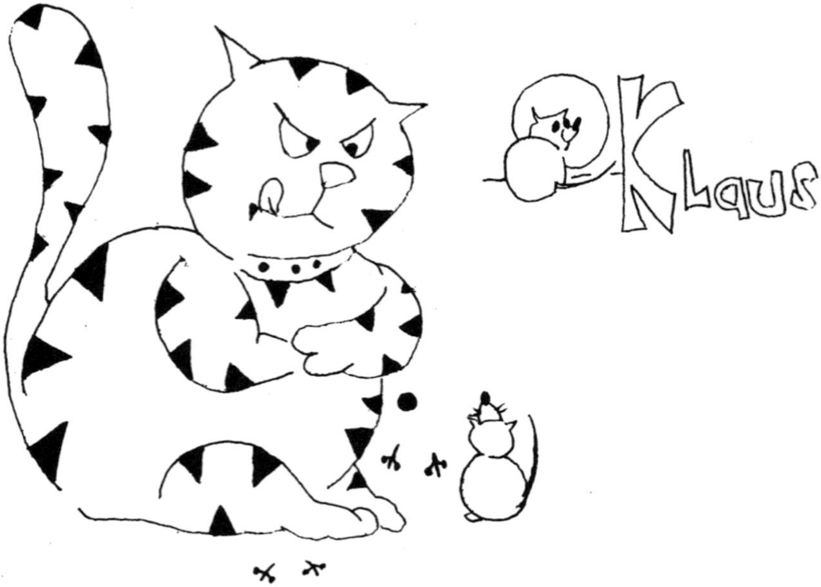
Klaus

Klaus The Mouse

There is a mouse that lives in my house. His name is Klaus. When little eyes stare up at me, I know it's Klaus, the little mouse.

At night, when I hear little feet, I know it's Klaus, the little mouse.

At break of day, screams came my way. I raced to the scene, and what did I see? Mary, my sister, was screaming at me. She stood on the top of the kitchen table. She would have climbed higher, had she been able. "It's Klaus, the mouse," she yelled my way.

My mother said, "Shoo!" and scared Klaus away.

The very next day, Mom got a cat that liked to eat rats, and Mary named him Max. Klaus and Max met under the table, and Klaus said to Max, "My name is Klaus, and I live in this house."

Max licked his lips. "My name is Max, and I'm here to eat rats. Are you a rat?"

"I'm not a rat, I'm a mouse named Klaus, and you're in my house."

"I'm sorry," said Max, who packed up some snacks, played with some jacks and stopped his attacks.

Mary still screams and jumps on the table.

Mom still buys cats that like to eat rats, and tiny feet still race up and down leaving tracks, and from under the table, little eyes still stare up at me.

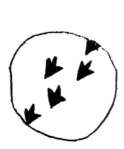

I know it's Klaus, that crafty mouse.

The End

EZRA ARARAT is a Bermudian who has always found relaxation and inspiration through writing. In high school, his teachers always complimented his vivid imagination. He benefited from their motivation, because his learning disability —possibly dyslexia—prevented him from excelling.

He credits his parents, Mr. & Mrs. Peter Trott, for supporting and believing in him, and he is thankful that God has blessed him with a photographic memory.

Ararat's guests at Coral Beach encouraged him to pursue his passion for writing. These stories are just a small example of his literary efforts, yet they reveal his great interest in young people and their welfare.

Ararat has four children: Ezra, Rene, Nicole and Ezra. He has certificates from Relais & Chateaux, the Department of Agriculture and Fisheries and the Bermuda International Youth Science. He also has obtained a GED.

In 1997, after presenting his stories to The Writers' Machine, Ezra was asked to take them back and polish them. He did so, and today is proud to know that his first major effort at writing will be an inspiration to Bermuda's children.

Rock Lessons are stories from Ararat's experiences. They reflect his insight into things great and small.

MARCUS TUCKER
Illustrator

Marcus Tucker was born on April 20, 1975 and is a graduate of the Bermuda College. He attended the Institute d'Adventiste du Sale've and Oakwood College. He enjoys art, poetry and music. This is his first book.

Marcus is currently a para-professional at Northlands Primary School.